SCHOOL SAFETY

Written by
Susan Kesselring

Illustrated by
Dan McGeehan

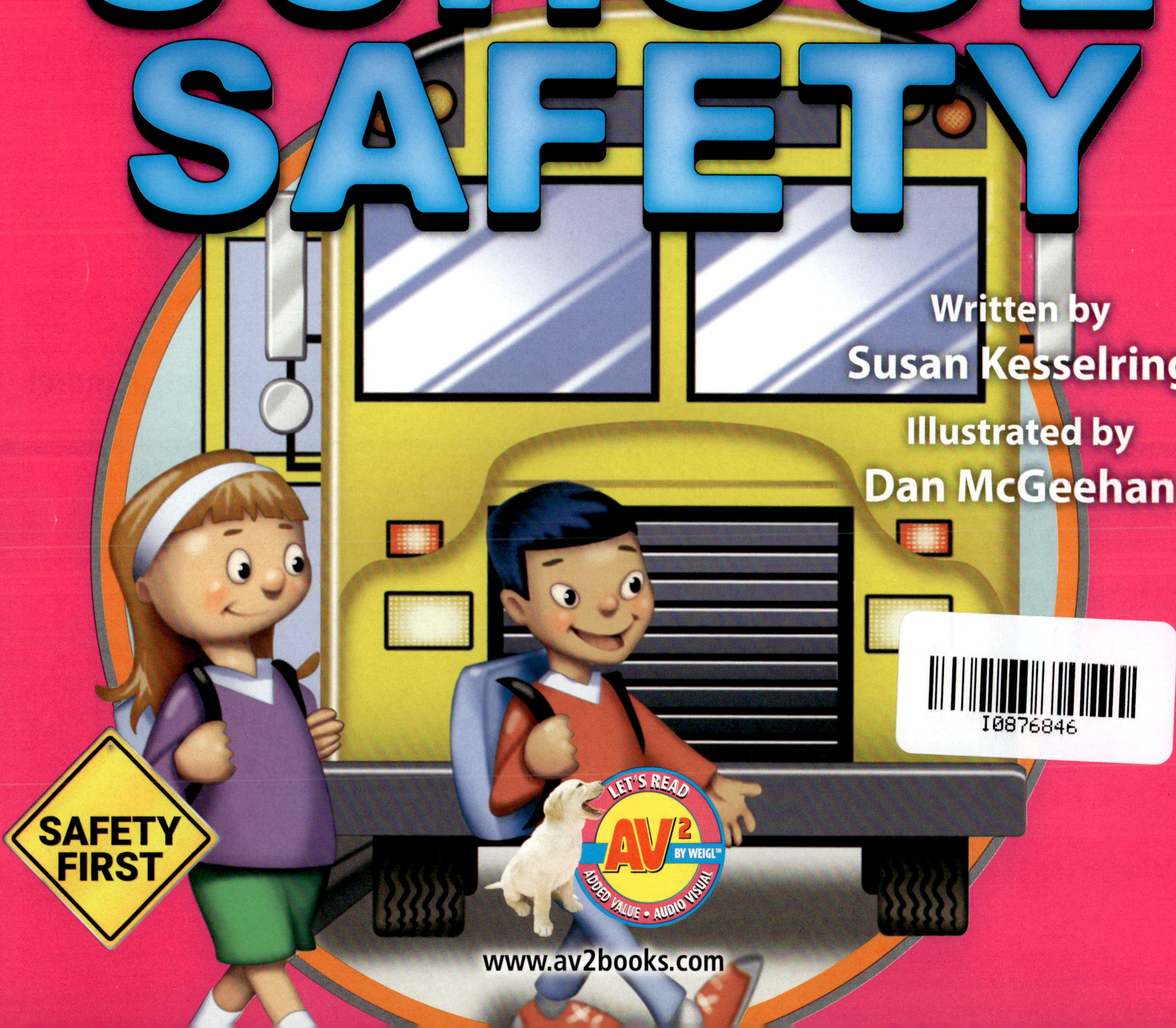

www.av2books.com

Go to **www.av2books.com**, and enter this book's unique code.

BOOK CODE

AVD53324

AV² by Weigl brings you media enhanced books that support active learning.

AV² provides enriched content that supplements and complements this book. Weigl's AV² books strive to create inspired learning and engage young minds in a total learning experience.

Your AV² Media Enhanced books come alive with...

Audio
Listen to sections of the book read aloud.

Video
Watch informative video clips.

Embedded Weblinks
Gain additional information for research.

Try This!
Complete activities and hands-on experiments.

Key Words
Study vocabulary, and complete a matching word activity.

Quizzes
Test your knowledge.

Slide Show
View images and captions, and prepare a presentation.

... and much, much more!

Published by AV² by Weigl
350 5th Avenue, 59th Floor New York, NY 10118
Website: www.av2books.com

Library of Congress Cataloging-in-Publication Data

Names: Kesselring, Susan, author.
Title: School safety / Susan Kesselring.
Description: New York, NY : AV² by Weigl, 2020. | Series: Safety first | Audience: K to Grade 3.
Identifiers: LCCN 2018053396 (print) | LCCN 2018055214 (ebook) | ISBN 9781489699657 (Multi User Ebook) | ISBN 9781489699664 (Single User Ebook) | ISBN 9781489699633 (hardcover : alk. paper) | ISBN 9781489699640 (softcover : alk. paper)
Subjects: LCSH: Schools--Safety measures--Juvenile literature. | Safety education--Juvenile literature.
Classification: LCC LB2864.5 (ebook) | LCC LB2864.5 .K47 2020 (print) | DDC 363.11/9371--dc23
LC record available at https://lccn.loc.gov/2018053396

Printed in the United States of America in Brainerd, Minnesota
1 2 3 4 5 6 7 8 9 0 22 21 20 19 18

112018
102918

Project Coordinator: Jared Siemens Designer: Ana María Vidal

First published by The Child's World in 2011

SCHOOL SAFETY

In this book, you will learn about

safety at school,

what to do,

what not to do,

and much more!

What is the best part of your school day? Is it riding the bus? Maybe it's swinging on the monkey bars at recess. Or do you love solving math problems?

School is a wonderful place to learn and have fun. But you need to watch out for a few things, too. Learn how to be safe and you will enjoy school even more!

SCHOOL
BUS
STOP

Hurry, it's time to catch the bus! Ask a parent to walk you to the bus stop and wait with you. Or, walk with friends. It's best to be with someone you know while waiting for the bus.

At your bus stop, watch out for traffic. Remember to stand on the sidewalk. You'll be safer a few feet away from the street.

Try to be at the bus stop at least five minutes before the bus is to arrive.

If you drop something by the side of the bus, tell your bus driver. He or she will let you know when it's safe to pick it up.

Can your bus driver see you outside the bus? Make eye contact with your bus driver so you know he or she has seen you.

If you have to walk in front of the bus to get on, stay five big steps from the bus. Stay two big steps away from the sides, except for when you're getting on and off.

Never walk behind the bus. Your bus driver cannot see you there.

If you leave something on the bus, do not go back to get it. Ask your bus driver about it the next time you ride the bus.

Once you are on the bus, find a seat right away. Face forward during the ride. Doing so will help keep you safe if there is an accident. Keep your feet and book bag out of the aisle so no one trips. Also, don't stick anything out the window. That includes your head and hands!

Your bus driver works hard to get you to school safely. Talk to your friends in a quiet voice. Loud voices can distract the driver.

Never let someone give you a ride to or from school unless it is okay with your parents.

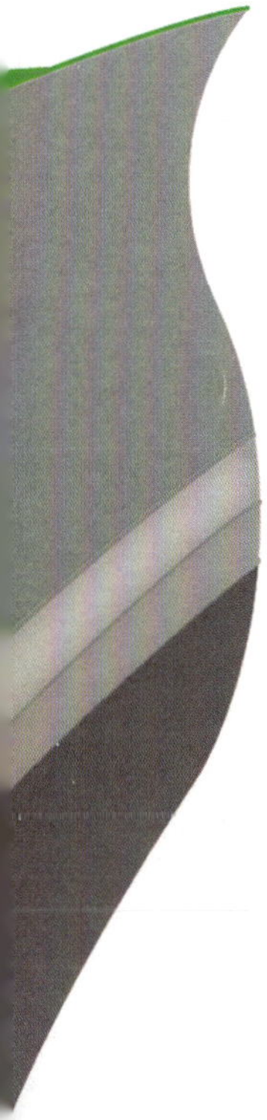

Do you like walking to school? It's great exercise. It's fun, too. Make sure you walk with a friend or a parent. If you ride your bike or scooter, wear a helmet.

Rain or snow can make a walk wet or cold. What's your plan for walking in bad weather? Ask your parents what to wear and what to do.

Your classroom is a pretty safe place to be. But watch out for things that could hurt someone. Sharp pencils and scissors can poke or seriously hurt people. Always carry them with the points facing down.

Keep the floor near your desk clear so no one trips. At your desk, sit straight in your chair. Avoid tipping it backward. You could fall and hurt your head.

If anyone hits or punches you, tell a teacher right away. If someone hurts your feelings, try to stay calm. Say, "I don't like that," and explain why.

If you're the one who hurt somebody else's feelings, apologize. Saying you're sorry takes a lot of courage, but you can do it.

Jungle gyms have been part of playgrounds for about 90 years!

It's time for recess! Are you ready to play ball and climb the jungle gym? Jungle gyms are fun, but almost half of all injuries on the playground happen on jungle gyms. It's very important to stay safe on the playground.

If you see something sharp or dangerous, stay away from it. Tell an adult who is outside with you. Avoid touching any animals, such as squirrels or birds. Look out for things you could trip over, too.

Use the swings as they are meant to be used. Only one person should sit on a swing at a time.

You've climbed up the ladder and are ready to slide! Wait for the person ahead of you to reach the ground before you go. You don't want to crash into someone! Always slide on your bottom, with your feet in front.

Can you go high on the swings? Be sure to sit on the seat. Wait until the swing stops before you get off. Be careful you don't get kicked as you pass by the front or back of the swings.

The bell is ringing. School's out! All your classmates are ready to leave. You may be in a hurry, but remember to walk. If you run, you could fall or bump someone else.

Tomorrow will be another day to learn and be safe!

KEY WORDS

Research has shown that as much as 65 percent of all written material published in English is made up of 300 words. These 300 words cannot be taught using pictures or learned by sounding them out. They must be recognized by sight. This book contains 136 common sight words to help young readers improve their reading fluency and comprehension. This book also teaches young readers several important content words, such as proper nouns.

Page	Sight Words First Appearance
4	at, day, do, is, it, it's, of, on, or, part, school, the, what, you, your
5	a, and, be, but, even, few, for, have, how, I, learn, me, more, need, out, place, tell, things, to, too, watch, will
7	ask, away, before, feet, from, know, stop, time, try, walk, while, with
8	by, he, if, let, she, side, something, up, when
9	big, can, eye, get, has, in, make, never, off, see, so, there, two
10	about, back, go, leave, next, not
11	also, an, are, book, don't, face, find, hands, hard, head, help, keep, no, once, one, right, talk, that, works
12	give
13	great, like
15	always, carry, could, down, near, people, points, them
17	say, takes, who, why
18	been, years
19	all, almost, animals, any, as, important, look, over, play, such, very
20	only, should, they, use
21	high, into, until, want
23	another, may, run

Page	Content Words First Appearance
4	bus, math, monkey bars, problems, recess
7	bus stop, friend, minutes, parent, sidewalk, street, traffic
8	bus driver
9	contact, steps
11	accident, aisle, book bag, ride, seat, window, voice
13	bike, exercise, helmet, rain, scooter, snow, weather
15	chair, classroom, desk, floor, pencils, scissors
17	courage, feelings, teacher
18	jungle gyms, playgrounds
19	adult, birds, injuries, squirrels
20	swings
21	bottom, ladder
23	bell, classmates